In the Name of Allah
the most *Gracious*
most Merciful

THE HERITAGE OF THE PETERBOROUGH BRITISH-PAKISTANI COMMUNITY IN PHOTOGRAPHS

Published by the Pakistan Community Association of Peterborough Raja Tahir Masood

ISBN: 978-0-9570333-3-7

Date: 15th April 2014

Website: www.british-pakistani.co.uk

Mobile: 07838624830

List of Publications by Raja Tahir Masood

- Home from Home – Hardback Published in October 2010

- The Heritage of Peterborough British-Pakistani Community -Paperback Published in October 2011

- The Heritage of Peterborough British-Pakistani Community - Paperback (junior edition) Published in December 2011

- Rags to Riches – Internet download (free) available since April 2012

- Lives and Quotes of World Famous People - Paperback Published in June 2013

Special Acknowledgement

To Heritage Lottery Fund for their financial support, Peterborough Museum for holding this exhibition, Peterborough City Council and Mohammad Akram Ayoub Choudhry for their donations.

Objectives

- To support the heritage, history of the Peterborough British-Pakistani community!

- To create awareness amongst the younger members of the British-Pakistani community of their heritage history.

- To foster a better understanding of the British-Pakistani community amongst other Peterborough communities!

- To promote community cohesion, encourage greater interaction and participation.

- To value, share and give recognition to the British-Pakistani community in their 60 year of active involvement in the development of Peterborough.

- To promote Peterborough as a welcoming, multicultural, vibrant, heritage, culture and a City of opportunity for all communities!

Thanks to Anees Lodhi, Ghulam Shabbir Awan, Ansar Ali, Gillian Beasley and Nazim Khan MBE for their assistance with the book

Preface

I have been privileged to write the Heritage of the Peterborough British-Pakistani Community in Photographs for the Pakistan Community Association of Peterborough. As far as I am aware, this is the first ever-comprehensive publication of this nature in 60 years.

All information is based on my knowledge, assessment & understanding of events and not knowingly influenced with aims to benefit any individual or organisation.

I have endeavoured to record all the important aspects of the community's heritage, that significance and relevance to the community.

Every effort is made to ensure that the book is in simple English, easy to read, including the creation of sub-headings to accommodate all sections of the community.

Al-Ghazzālī said:

> "Knowledge exists potentially in the human
> soul like the seed in the soil; by learning, the
> potential becomes actual"

I have made every effort to ensure that the book's print is of high quality but as you can appreciate that technology has greatly improved since many of the earliest photographs' were taken.

For cultural reasons, I encountered severe difficulties in obtaining photographs and profiles from the women members of the community and despite my efforts, few women have provided profiles and even fewer women agreed to have their photographs published.

Finally, I hope this book will become a recorded heritage, history of the Peterborough British-Pakistani community and that the earliest photographed personalities will be considered pioneers of the community in Peterborough.

Foreword

Peterborough in 2014 is a diverse city with many people from different backgrounds living here and the Pakistani community is one of the oldest and most established.

The first members of the Pakistani community arrived in Peterborough in the 1950s and saw it as "a city of opportunity with good employment prospects".

The Pakistani community has also played a key role in getting Peterborough to where it is today and where it will be tomorrow. If you take a trip around the city, you will see the Pakistani community's influence in many places, on the high street, in the business sector, in schools and communities and on this council.

The Heritage of the Peterborough British-Pakistani Community in Photographs offers a thoughtful and moving account of how the Pakistani community came to be in Peterborough and who the well-known characters were.

This history is complimented by some wonderful pictures of people and places from years gone by.

It is a fascinating read, particularly for those interested in the cultural modern history of a city we are all proud of.

Gillian Beasley
Chief Executive
Peterborough City Council

CONTENTS

The World Wars

In both World Wars Indian troops played an important role, especially the large number of Muslim soldiers who made up about a third of the old British Indian army originating from the integral areas of Pakistan and Kashmir. The Muslim soldiers were known for their reliability as steady dependable men.

The first Indian-born man awarded the Victoria Cross (VC) was Khudadad Khan. He was born in 1887 in the Village Dabb district of Mianwali in the state of Punjab.

When the First World War broke out, he joined the Army as a Private and served with the 129th (Duke of Connaught's Own) Baluchis as a machine gunner. In October 1914, his regiment was sent to the front line in France to help exhausted British troops. The Germans pushed the Baluchis back and all the gunners were killed apart from Khan. He was badly wounded, but still prevented the German Army from reaching vital ports and for his matchless feat of courage and gallantry, 26-year old Khan performed an act of bravery for which he was awarded the Victoria Cross (VC). He was the first ever Indian-born person to receive this honour. Khan died on 8th March 1971.

In the First World War the Indians, Muslims who served with the British Indian force numbered approximately 400,000.

In the Second World War, one of the most renowned soldiers was Abdul Hafiz. He was born in 1915 in a village Kalanaur in the state of Punjab. He served with the ninth Jat Regiment of the Indian Army and led an attack against the Japanese forces in the north of Imphal in Burma (Myanmar). Their regiment met with strong resistance, Hafiz was wounded, but still continued to attack enemy positions and killed several of their soldiers. Later he was fatally wounded by Japanese machine-gun fire and he died on 6th April 1944. Abdul Hafiz was posthumously awarded the Victoria Cross (VC).

Muslim women also played their parts in both wars and one notable example of this was Noor Inayat Khan a Special Operations Executive (SOE). Born on 1st January 1914 in Moscow, her father was the great-grandson of the Tipu Sultan of Mysore. In November 1942, she joined F (France) (SOE). On 13th October 1943, Nazis arrested Noor and brutally tortured her; and on 13th September 1944, they executed her aged 30. Noor is mentioned in Dispatches and was awarded the French

Cross of War with a Gold Star and a Member of British Empire (MBE) as well as posthumously being awarded the George Cross.

In 1945 the recorded number of Indian Muslim soldiers was 832,500.

Post-War Britain

In Britain after the Second World War new employment opportunities opened up for migrants. Britain's economy set off for a long post-war economic expansion and had an acute shortage of labour.

Poverty

In the 1940's and 50's unemployment and poverty were high in the Mirpur district in Azad Jammu and Kashmir, people were, finding life a daily struggle and were in search of any employment opportunities in an efforts to improve their lives.

Migration to Peterborough

Enticed by the employment opportunities and financial gains first direct migration commenced in 1950s from villages and towns of the Mirpur district, (Kotli and Bhimber were sub-divisions of the Mirpur district at that time), in Azad Jammu and Kashmir and from the province of Punjab in Pakistan villages of Sarai Alamgir and the town of Gujar Khan to Peterborough.

Finances

Many migrants had difficulties in raising finances and often several family members pooled their savings in an effort to raise the sufficient funds, to enable one person from a family to travel to Britain.

Migrant Goals

Every new migrant arrived in the UK with the intention of working hard and saving enough funds to be able to return to Pakistan. Their planned goals were to create small businesses, construct new houses, purchase land or initiate other projects, which would create employment opportunities, generate income and make their lives comfortable. The reality was that they were living a utopia and there was no turning back, signifying the start of permanent migration.

Accommodation

On their arrival into Peterborough, the new migrants were dependent on local resident for their accommodation. According to the surviving elders, their landlords frequently imposed restrictions on their lodging terms, for example not allowing them to cook or consume spicy food in the houses or permit visitors.

Curiosity

Being few in numbers, the local population often treated them as subjects of curiosity. Every early surviving migrant has a story to share and some were even asked if they washed their faces, whether the brown colour of their skin would also wash off!

Language

The new migrants encountered severe difficulties in sustaining daily lives that was due to their poor command of English and it related to their levels of education, as most were either illiterate or had only acquired a basic education in Pakistan. However, they were resourceful people and managed to survive by seeking assistance from the educated members of the community and the assisting members felt obliged to help them.

Climate

The new migrants found the British climate cold and different from the warmer conditions they were familiar with in Pakistan, but they quickly adapted to the change, viewed new opportunities with an enthusiasm and desire to succeed.

Unemployed

A large number of migrants also experienced problems with unemployment. Whilst unemployed their relatives assumed responsibilities for their upkeep and without any paybacks. The unemployed also expected that their relations would maintain them. To assist the unemployed relations actively made efforts to find them employment. But they were resilient people and not deterred by unemployment, many travelled from town to town in the hope of securing employment. Every employed person worked hard to accomplished good record as many felt insecure about finding alternative employment. Thus, high numbers worked for the same employer and some for up to 30 to 40 years.

Priorities

After securing employment, migrants budgeted to pay for their relatives in Pakistan to join them in the UK. This was to ensure that other family members also benefitted from the new economic opportunities.

Diet

The migrants faced a restrictive diet as no halal meat or spices were available locally, members were dependent on live poultries sold at the Cattle Market. Some numbers travelled to the nearby Cities of Nottingham and Leicester to buy their essentials until late Chaudhry Mohammed Aurangzeb established a shop on Cromwell Road in early 60's.

Racism

Another major problem migrant faced was with direct racism, where they were racially abused, intimidated, threatened and often physically attacked. The earliest generations were very law-abiding, non-confrontational people and they accepted that racism was part of their everyday life.

Comfort Zone

Once the community had grown in population, a few entrepreneurial members purchased their own dwellings in the Gladstone Area and invited other relations to lodge with them. This move was popular with the community and resulted, in some cases, in numbers as high as 25 - 30 occupants in one house. Many people preferred to live with their relations and found that community and family links provided them with a comfort zone. It also eased their transition into a new environment and, helped to save funds. These early generations presented themselves as honest, caring, considerate, reliable, flexible, helpful and hardworking people.

Employment Prospects

According to the earliest arrivals, Peterborough was renowned for its good employment prospects in the Brickyard industry, Perkins Engines and other small foundries. Migrants were often employed in unskilled, low paid, noisy and demanding jobs. Many worked in permanent night and worked from 12 -16 hours a shift, earning £5-£6 a week. They walked several kilometres (sometimes even up to 15 kilometres) to and from work, they were resilient and high-spirited people and nothing seemed impossible to them.

Family

The migrants were in regular contact with their families in Pakistan by letters as well as providing with finances. Almost all migrants visited their families in Pakistan in every three to four years. The majorities were married with young children and stayed with their families in Pakistan for several months and while in Pakistan everyone constructed new houses and others purchased land.

First Arrival

I felt the best way to identify the first arrival in the City would be to inspect the Electoral Registers, the first community member's name that appears on the Register, is Noogrn Mohammad and Kluzir Mohammad at 110 Russell Street registered in 1958/59. The following year the Electoral Registration from the same address was registered under the name of Mohammed Suleman. I have spoken with Haji Mohammed Suleman and he has confirmed that he purchased the house from Chaudhry Fakeer Mohammed and he believes that the couple moved to Peterborough in 1954.

Although I am aware that most early arrivals were illiterate or probably unsure about the Electoral Registration process, my evidence is based on written information therefore I am happy to confirm that Noogrn Mohammed alias Chaudhry Fakeer Mohammed from Kotli in Azad Kashmir, was indeed the first Pakistani to arrive in Peterborough.

Sharing Experience

Mohammed Nazir shared his experience of arriving in Peterborough with us. According to Mohammed Nazir he arrived in Peterborough in May 1958 with two other friends Fazal Hussain and Mohammed Yaqoob. A mutual friend provided them with transport from Bedford and he told them that Peterborough was a City of opportunities with good employment prospects. Unfortunately, the three had only been in the country for a short period and were unfamiliar as to how to acquire accommodation. At nightfall, without any other options, the three spent their first night in the town centre under the historic Guildhall building.

Their second night was spent in the railway station waiting room. On the third day, out of sheer desperation, they headed towards the nearest residential area, Cromwell Road and knocked on residential doors and asked for living accommodation. Luckily all three manage to find accommodation individually.

Father's Experience

My late father Haji Anayat Ali from the village of Morah Bari in Mirpur, Azad Jammu and Kashmir was also amongst the early arrivals in the City in 1959. Father first arrived in Sheffield in 1958, and a few months later moved to Nottingham in search of employment and several months later came to Peterborough. He was employed by the London Brick Yard company as a truck driver and lodged with an Italian family in Stanground.

Mosques

In the mid 1960s, the community population had grown considerably and some prominent community activist decided to establish a Mosque. They purchased a detached residential building on Cromwell Road for £2,800 and with council permission converted it into a Mosque. To finance the Mosque building, every employed community member was asked to donate one-week's wages toward the Mosque funds, they all happily followed the appeal instruction and in 1967, the first Peterborough City Mosque was established on Cromwell Road.

The Hussaini Islamic Centre

The first Hussaini Islamic Centre was established on Burton Street in 1975 and due to the increasing population, the community built their first purpose Mosque with a small dome in 1992, with the capacity for 550 people.

Ghousia Mosque

In 1981, another detached residential building was purchased at Gladstone Street for £24,000 and with council permission converted into the Ghousia Mosque.

Dar-as-Salaam Mosque

In 1997, a former hotel building with considerable land on Alma Road was purchased for £110,000 and with council permission converted into the Dar-as-Salaam Mosque.

Faizan-e-Madinah Mosque

In 2000, Cromwell Road Mosque committee members went through an extensive wave of consultations with the community to ascertain their views on the newly proposed Faizan-e-Madinah Mosque. The community unanimously endorsed the new Mosque proposal and immediately started their donations. Work commenced on the Faizan-e-Madinah Mosque in December 2001 at a new site on Gladstone Street and Link Road and was completed in 2006. The Faizan-e-Madinah Mosque has a capacity of 3,000 people and costs three million pounds.

New Ghousia Mosque

In 2002, work commenced on the new Ghousia Mosque on an adjacent site of the old Ghousia Mosque at Gladstone Street and was completed in 2004, costing £1.4 million and with the capacity for 1,200 people.

Masjid Khadijah & Islamic Centre

In 2008, refurbishment and extension work started on the Masjid Khadijah & Islamic Centre at Cromwell Road and completed in 2010, costing £250,000 with a capacity for 450 people.

Dar-as-Salaam Mosque

In 2009, building work began in phases on a new Dar-as-Salaam Mosque, with 500 people capacity at an estimated cost of one million pounds.

Community Centres

In the late 1970s, Peterborough, South Asian communities acquired the Asian Cultural Centre building on Lincoln Road New England from Peterborough City Council to meet the growing community needs with provision for young people. The building was an old church converted into a community centre it had old wooden floors and very basic facilities. In 1989, Peterborough City Council built a new 1.2 million pound Gladstone Park Community Centre to meet the local British-Pakistani community needs with adequate provision for young people.

Population

In the 2001, census the British-Pakistani community population in Peterborough was just under 6,000. In 2011, the census population was 12,078 and now the estimated population is 15,000.

Gladstone Area

For the last 60 years, the Gladstone Area has been the established base of the Peterborough British-Pakistani community, but in recent years, the community has become prosperous and their needs have become greater resulting in high numbers of residents moving into other City areas.

British-Pakistani population in the UK

Year	Population
2014	1,400,000 Estimated
2011	1,125,000
2001	750,000
1991	480,000
1981	300,000
1971	120,000
1961	25,000
1951	10,000

Some well-known British-Pakistani figures in the UK

- Amir Iqbal Khan is a professional boxer. He is a former two-time World Champion by winning WBA, WBA (Super) and IBF Light Welterweight. Amir Khan was the youngest British Olympic boxing medallist in 2004.
- James Caan (formerly Nazim Khan) is an entrepreneur and television personality. He is best known as a former investor on the BBC's programme Dragons' Den.
- Baroness Sayeeda Warsi was appointed a life peer in 2007. She was the Co-Chairman of the Conservative Party. Now appointed Senior Minister of State for Foreign and Commonwealth Affairs in the Foreign and Commonwealth Office and Minister for Faith and Communities.
- Sir Anwar Pervez is a businessman and one of the richest Asians in UK.

He is the founder of the Bestway Group and a self-made owner of companies worth billions of pounds.

♦ Lord Nazir Ahmed is a member of the House of Lords and the second Muslim life peer.

Prosperity

Since the closure of old heavy industries, new opportunities have opened up for the entrepreneurial members of the community. Many members have seized new opportunities and become prosperous through various businesses, for example, second-hand car garages, property letting management, insurance brokers and workforce recruitment agencies. The community's numbers have also increased in other established professions likes accountancy and law.

Mirpur

It is now estimated that 70% of the British-Pakistani population in UK are of Mirpuri descent. Mirpur is a small district in Azad Jammu and Kashmir, Pakistan. Traditionally, the inhabitants of Mirpur district were small landowning farmers, dependent on seasonal crops and livestock, whilst younger men served in the army.

Integration

Younger members of the British-Pakistani community often resent this word and simply think it creates a one-sided focus on minority communities. There is also a widespread view in the community regardless of their efforts that the indigenous community will never accept them as being truly British. Some members of the British-Pakistani community are critical of the low levels of awareness and general lack of interest in the indigenous community regarding minority communities and cultures. Other members recognise that their community will have to compromise parts of their culture in the process of integrating.

Drugs, Crime and Prison

The consumption and trade of drugs has been on the rise amongst the younger members of the community. Often their first exposure comes after leaving school without any formal qualifications and then encountering severe difficulties in gaining employment, which leads to frustrations and ultimately result in becoming caught up in drugs. Their initial involvement starts as consumers, but the cost and a desire to get rich quick often changes to into suppliers. The young people's actions are distressing their parents and having a detrimental impact on the British-Pakistani community as a whole. Many parents feel confused as to why their sons have become involved with drugs, unsure as to whom to approach for help. They feel powerless to persuade them and some families even send their sons on a long 'holiday' to Pakistan in the hope that a change of environment will lead to a cessation in drug use.

Sadly, many young people have become dependent on drugs, drug addiction is a costly habit, and one of the ways they feed their addiction is to turn to low-level crime. Their unlawful activities led to prosecutions, court convictions and prison. In 1991, there were 1,959 Muslims in UK prisons, and in 1999, the number had more than doubled, with 4,335 in prison. In 2012, there were 11,248 Muslim prisoners in England and Wales 13% of the total prison population of about 85,000, when the Muslim population in the UK is about 5% of the total population. I am aware that these figures do include a proportion of prisoners who have converted to Islam whilst in prison.

Arranged Marriages

Traditionally, all marriages in the British-Pakistani community were arranged by the families within local areas or the same clans, but there has been a cultural shift amongst young people, who feel a reluctance to follow their parents' footsteps marrying into families or in Pakistan. Many of these young people's actions are leading to clashes and severe resentments within their families and long-term family fallouts.

In recent years, a high percentage of parents' attitudes are changing and many have started to embrace the time related changes, often permitting the wishes of their children in order to avoid divisions in family. However, there are still a number of parents who find the cultural related changes difficult to accept, which leads to tensions and other problems in their families.

Racism

Members of the British-Pakistani population do not openly tolerate racism and will challenge racists, but sadly, the reality is that they still experience racism and prejudice in the form of race hate and indirect racism. Race hate can range from racist graffiti on buildings to verbal abuse and physical attacks. Indirect racism is where people suffer daily discrimination in their work place; this includes disproportionate competition for employment, training, pay and promotion.

Discontent

Young people from the British-Pakistani community are constantly asking who represents their views and this is because they often feel ignored by the establishments, and politicians. The area, which frustrates the young people most, is Britain's stance on foreign policy and they view our current policies from unfair, unbalanced and to dishonest. Most young people strongly believe that if Britain follows a course that is more systematic and principled then in the long term Britain will gain more respect around the world.

Conclusion

The majority of British-Pakistani community members are British by birth and almost all others have British nationalities; despite varying experiences of racism, poverty and other social inequalities, the British-Pakistani community truly believes it has a strong and indispensable connection with Britain.

In Peterborough, the community has grown from a small group of migrants to become one of the largest minorities embedded and established community. Members of the community are constantly aspiring to improve their quality of lives with an increasing population becoming prosperous.

Peterborough City Centre in 1900

The Heritage of the Community

The first Pakistani to have arrived in Peterborough was the late
Chaudhry Fakeer Mohammed of Kotli in Azad Jammu and Kashmir

The Heritage of the Community

Mohammed Amin son of late Chaudhry Arshad Ahmed of Kalyal Bainsi, Mirpur was amongst the earliest children to have arrived in Peterborough

The Heritage of the Community

Late Haji Anayat Ali of Morah Bari, Mirpur and
late Haji Mohammed Fazil of Karie, Mirpur

The Heritage of the Community

Abdul Rahman formally of Sehotha, Dhoke Hail, Mirpur

Late Haji Fazal Karim of Potha Bainsi, Mirpur

The Heritage of the Community

Late Chaudhry Muhammed Sarwar of Chori, Kotli

The Heritage of the Community

Chaudhry Tikka Khan of Kalyal Bainsi with his late uncle Chaudhry Mohammed Sadiq of Kalyal Bainsi, Mirpur

Brothers late Mohammed Aslam and Haji Mohammed Afzal of Dina

The Heritage of the Community

Late Haji Karamat Hussain of Kandthill, Mirpur

The Heritage of the Community

Ghulam Shabbir Awan with his late father Malik Khadim Hussain
of Gujar Khan

The Heritage of the Community

Late Haji Chaudhry Rahmat Khan of Orangabad, Saria Alimgir

Late Haji Khadam Hussain of Potha Bainsi, Mirpur

Haji Alam Din of Rakhyal, Morah Lohran, Mirpur

The Heritage of the Community

Haji Mohammed Zaman of Sang, Mirpur
The Heritage of the Community

Late Haji Chaudhry Abdul Aziz of Juna, Kotli

Late Mohammed Najib Ratyal formally of Bandur, Mirpur

Late Haji Mardan Ali of Sarai Alamgir

The Heritage of the Community

Late Haji Karamat Hussain (President) of Potha Bainsi, Mirpur

The Heritage of the Community

Mohammed Nazir of Kalyal Bainsi, Mirpur

The Heritage of the Community

Late Haji Mohammed Ismail of Morah Bari, Mirpur

The Heritage of the Community

Above late
Qudrutullah Lodhi
formally of Sehotha,
Mirpur with late
Sardar Mohammed
Ibrahim Khan
and late Kurshid
Ahmed Lodhi
formally of Sehotha,
Mirpur.

Below late Sardar
Mohammed
Ibrahim Khan

The Heritage of the Community

Late Haji Munshi Khan Malik of Chak Saralian, Kotli

Haji Mirza Fazal Ali of Mirpur City

Late Chaudhry Arshad Ahmed of Kalyal Bainsi, Mirpur

The Heritage of the Community

Haji Mohammed Lal formally of Momnal, Mirpur

Late Haji Mohammed Sadiq of Kotian in Sarai Alamgir

The Heritage of the Community

Malik Muhammad Saqlain of Gujar Khan

Muhammad Zafran Awan of Gujar Khan

The Heritage of the Community

Late Raja
Moazam Khan
formally of
Batli, Mirpur

Mohammed
Shafiq of Lahore

Former St Pauls School (now close down) pupils
enjoying an away trip in 1978

Old Mirpur City being dismantled
The Heritage of the Community

Abdul Qayyum Malik of Chak Saralian, Kotli
The Heritage of the Community

Abdul Majeed formally of Morah Phagotian, Mirpur

The Heritage of the Community

Raja Ghazanfar Ali of Malot, Bhimber

The Heritage of the Community

Tariq Mahmood, Raja Akhtar Hussain and Khalid Masaud
all from Potha Bainsi, Mirpur

Abdul Qayyum
Malik of Chak
Saralian, Kotli

Mohammed Ayub of Sarai Alamgir and Shabir Ahmed Mirza of Mirpur City

The Heritage of the Community

Late Haji
Chaudhry Noor
Mohammed
with his son
Chaudhry
Mohammed
Rashid of Kala
Dabb, Kotli

Mohammed
Amin of
Kalyal
Bainsi,
Mirpur

The Heritage of the Community

Late Chaudhry Arshad Ahmed of Kalyal Bainsi, Mirpur

The Heritage of the Community

Babu Mohammed Yousaf of Palahal Kalan, Kotli

Javed Rehman Mirza of Mirpur City and Habib-ur-Rahman formally of Luddar, Mirpur

Shabir Ahmed Mirza of Mirpur City

The Heritage of the Community

Late
Mohammed
Rasheed, Tariq
Mahmood and
Raja Akhtar
Hussain of
Potha Bainsi,
Mirpur

Chaudhry Mohammed Rashid of Kala Dabb, Kotli

The Heritage of the Community

Raja Sakandar Khan formally of Damyal, Mirpur, Mohammed Nadim and
Raja Mohammed Sabir (Kakra) of Potha Bainsi, Mirpur

Late Haji
Chaudhry
Maqbool
Hussain of
Kanily, Mirpur

The Heritage of the Community

Mohammed Ayub of Marha Khai in Mirpur and Mohammerd Najib of Morah Bari, Mirpur

Shakil Irfan of Morah Bari, Mirpur

The Heritage of the Community

Dr Brian Mawhinny MP, Jannifer Suri, late Manga Khan of Chak Haryam late Qudrutullah Lodhi of Sehotha, Abdul Aziz of Potha Bainsi and late Kurshid Ahmed Lodhi of Sehota all from Mirpur

Pakistan Community Association organised Qwali function at Gladstone Park Community Centre in early 1990's

The Heritage of the Community

Shafiq Ahmed Mirza of Mirpur City

Mohammed Shahzad of Islamgarh, Mirpur

The Heritage of the Community

Ansar Ali, Raja Tahir Masood, Councillor Nazim Khan MBE, with late Dr
Ayub Thakur a Prominent Kashmiri figure from Srinagar and Raja Akhtar
Hussain all from Mirpur

Raja
Mohammed
Sabir (Kakra)
of   Potha
Bainsi,
Mirpur and
Habib-ur-
Rahman
formally of
Luddar,
Mirpur

Late Haji
Mohammed
Sajwal of Kanily,
Mirpur

Raja Akhtar
Hussain of Potha
Bainsi, Mirpur

The Heritage of the Community

Late Haji Fazal Karim of Potha Bainsi, Mirpur and late Moalna Mustafa of
Ahmedabad, India

The Heritage of the Community

Ansar Ali of Rakhyal, Morah Lohran, Mirpur

The Heritage of the Community

Muzaffar-ul-Hassan of Sarai Alamgir visiting Ajmeer, India

Haji Aurangzeb Khan of Islamgarh , Mirpur

The Heritage of the Community

67

Former Peterborough Mayor Mohammad Akram Ayoub Choudhary
of Khanka Katara, Kotli

The Heritage of the Community

Ansar Ali of Rakhyal, Morah Lohran, Mirpur

The Heritage of the Community

69

Late Hafiz of Abdul Malik of Chitterpuri, Mirpur

Late Haji Khadeem Hussain of Potha Bainsi, Mirpur

The Heritage of the Community

Haji Mohammed Afzal of Dina

Mohammad Akram Ayoub Choudhary of Khanka Katra, Kotli on Mayoral
duties

The Heritage of the Community

71

Late Haji Shah Mohammed of Kanily, Mirpur

Raja Tahir Masood (Author) of Morah Bari, Mirpur

The Heritage of the Community

72

Mohammad Akram Ayoub Choudhary of Khanka Katara, Kotli
on his Mayoral duties with Mubbarak Mawani and Daphne Ward

Mohammad Akram Ayoub Choudhary of Khanka Katara, Kotli with the
former British Prime Minister Tony Blair
The Heritage of the Community

Late
Chaudhry
Mohammed
Aurangzeb
formally of
Batli, Mirpur

Haji Mohammed Sulman of Kanily, Mirpur

The Heritage of the Community

Former Mayor of Peterborough Raja Akhtar Hussain of Potha Bainsi, Mirpur

The Heritage of the Community

Late Haji Mohammed Zakria of Saria Alamgir with his son Muzaffar-ul-Hassan
The Heritage of the Community

Haji Swar Khan formally of Neele, Mirpur

The Heritage of the Community

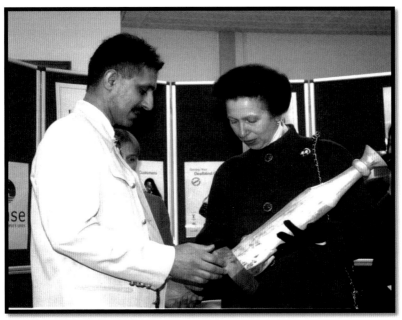

Abdullah Abdul Majid of Kanily, Mirpur with Princess Ann

Late Mohammed Sarwar Rija of Punjab, Pakistan

The Heritage of the Community

Late Ghulam
Yousaf Kayani
of Jelhum

Late Chaudhry
Maqbool
Hussain of
Kanily, Mirpur

The Heritage of the Community

Raja Mohammed Sabir (Kakra) of Potha Bainsi, Mirpur

The Heritage of the Community

Abdul Waheed of Sang, Mirpur
The Heritage of the Community

Late Haji Anayat Ali of Morah Bari, Mirpur

The Heritage of the Community

Javed Ahmed
of Jaurahabad
and formally
from Mirpur

Cllr Nazim Khan MBE of Kalyal Bainsi with David Miliband former British
Foreign Secretary along with Raja Mohammed Sabir (Kakra) of Kara Town
and Abdul Majid of Kalyal Bainsi all from Mirpur

The Heritage of the Community

Haji Mirza Fazal
Ali of Mirpur City

Choudhry Mohammed Rashid of Kala Dabb, Kotli with his sons
Irfan, Usman and Kamran Rashid

The Heritage of the Community

Khalid
Mahmood
Junvee of Juna
Bal, Kotli

Mohammed
Khan of
Khanka Katra,
Kotli

The Heritage of the Community

Haji Mohammed Walayat of Morah Bari, Mirpur

Tahir Jamil
of Morah
Bari, Mirpur

The Heritage of the Community

Raja Tahir Masood (Author) of Morah Bari, Mirpur at the launch of his The
Heritage of Peterborough British-Pakistani-Community book in October 2011
The Heritage of the Community

Raja Tahir Masood (Author) with Gillian Beasley the Chief Executive
of Peterborough City Council

Raja Tahir
Masood (Author)
with Cllr Nazim
Khan MBE of
Kalyal Bainsi,
Mirpur

Mohammad
Ayoub Choudhary
of Khanka Katara,
Kotli

Raja Tahir Masood (Author) with Cllr Nabil Ahmed Shabbir of Gujar Khan

The Heritage of the Community

Brothers Haji Mohammed Jamil and late Chaudhry Mohammed
Anwar formally of Batli, Mirpur

Haji Mohammed Khan formally of Sehotha, Mirpur

The Heritage of the Community

Raja Tahir Masood (Author) presenting some of his books to Sohail Sarfraz

Shahid Nawaz of Kakra Town, Mirpur

The Heritage of the Community

Shahid Hussain
of Kalyal Bainsi,
Mirpur

Raja
Ghazanfar
Ali of
Malot,
Bhimber

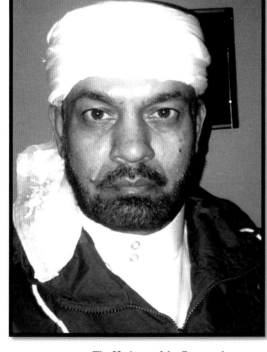

The Heritage of the Community

Shaukat Farid of
Charhoi, Kotli

Murad Ali of
Kakra Town,
Mirpur

The Heritage of the Community

Abdullah Abdul
Majid of Kanily,
Mirpur

Shahid Anwar of
Sarai Alamgir

The Heritage of the Community

Cllr Mohammed Jamil of Khanka Katara, Kotli

Ali Ditta of
Sang, Mirpur

The Heritage of the Community

Raja Saeed
Khan of
Karie, Mirpur

Saj Bashir
of Kakra
Town,
Mirpur

The Heritage of the Community

Deputy Mayor, Cllr Mohammed Nadeem of Parkodi, Mirpur

The Heritage of the Community

Haji Mohammed Ajaib formally of ludder, Mirpur

Barkat Ullah Shaikh of Sindh Province, Pakistan

The Heritage of the Community

Ghulam Shabbir Awan of Gujar Khan

Mohammed Shabir of Faisalabad formally from Mirpur

Raja Tahir Masood (Author) presenting some of his books to Sardar Attique Ahmed Khan

Dr Muhammed Ikram Choudhry, Bhimber
The Heritage of the Community

Mohammed Farooq of Naka, Mirpur

Rezwan Ali
of Jhelum

The Heritage of the Community

Mohammed
Mansha of
Palahal Kalan,
Kotli

Yasir
Mahmood of
Chakar,
Muzaffarabad

The Heritage of the Community

Shabir
Ahmed
Mirza from
Mirpur City

Sajad Majid
of Mandi
Bahauddin
formally
from Mirpur

The Heritage of the Community

Late Mohammed Shabir of Mara Omar, Mirpur

Sajid Mahmood of Kalyal Bainsi, Mirpur

The Heritage of the Community

Babu
Mohammed
Hussain of
Khanka Katar,
Kotli

Waseem Jamil of Khanka Katara, Kotli
The Heritage of the Community

Mohammed Shahzad of Islamgarh, Mirpur

Mohsin Tulhat of Sarai Alamgir

The Heritage of the Community

Mohammed Younis of Kanily, Mirpur

Keyz Bashir of Kakra Town, Mirpur

The Heritage of the Community

Choudhry
Maqbool
Hussain of
Kanily, Mirpur

Qadeer Karim of Khari Sharif, Mirpur
The Heritage of the Community

Ghafarat Shahid Palahal Kalan, Kotli

Shaukat Farid of Charhoi, Kotli

The Heritage of the Community

Asif
Rahman of
Dhangria,
Mirpur

Rahman
Ahmed
Qureshi of
Saria
Alimgir

The Heritage of the Community

Mohammed Shafiq and his father, Habib-ur-Rahman formally of Luddar, Mirpur

Kamraiz
Akhtar of
Kandthill,
Mirpur

The Heritage of the Community

Sardar Raja Ghulam Abbas Vains of formally of Momnal from Mirpur and now residing at Mandi Bahauddin living in Peterborough

Zahid Akbar of Palahal Kalan, Kotli

Late Mohammed Abu Bakr Ahmed of Chak Haryam, Mirpur

The Heritage of the Community

Abdul Aziz
Choudhary of
Parahi, Kotli

Ch Ali Shan of Kanily, Mirpur
The Heritage of the Community

Zafar Iqbal
Mirza of
Mirpur City

Tariq Iqbal
Mirza of Mirpur
City

The Heritage of the Community

Raja Tariq
Jamil of
Khanka
Katara, Kotli

Israr Ahmed
of Kalyal
Bainsi,
Mirpur

The Heritage of the Community

Late Raja Munawar Khan formally of Damyal, Mirpur

Raja Sabeel Ahmed of Potha Bainsi, Mirpur

The Heritage of the Community

Amjid Hameed of Islamgarh, Mirpur

Raja Tahir Masood (Author) presenting one of his books to Abdul Rashid Turabi

The Heritage of the Community

Mohammed Shamim of Parkodi, Mirpur

Raja Fayyaz Khan of Kakra Town, Mirpur

The Heritage of the Community

Mrs Rubina Ishrat Hussain MBE with her husband late Haji Karamat Hussain of Potha Baini, Mirpur

In 2010 after the Pakistan Community Association AGM

Summer School facilitated at Ghousia Mosque

Ghousia Mosque Committee, in presence of Mohammed Sarwar former MP
of Glasgow Govan and current Governor of Punjab, Pakistan

The Heritage of the Community

Raja Liaquat Hussain of Gulyana, Gujar Khan

The Heritage of the Community

Muhammad
Ruksar of
Barjun, Mirpur

Raja Tahir Masood, Cllr Mohammed Azad, Ansar Ali and Raja Mohammed
Sabir (Kakra) all from Mirpur

The Heritage of the Community

Haji Aurangzeb Khan of Islamgarh, Mirpur

The Heritage of the Community

Altaf Hussain of Khari, Mirpur with his boxing trainers in Lond

Pakistan Youth Association Members Indoor Football Team

The Heritage of the Community

Altaf Hussain of Kharik, Mirpur as a member of GB Boxing team

Asian Youth Club Sunday League Football Team in 1980's

Ansar Ali was a member of Peter Brotherhood competition winning football team

The Heritage of the Community

Muzaffar-ul-Hussain with his trophy winning cricket team

Altaf Hussain with his son Gohir Altaf and trainers at a boxing gym

The Heritage of the Community

Young people celebrating Pakistan Cricket team victory

Pakistan Youth Association Members at the Peterborough United Football
Match

The Heritage of the Community

First Mosque in Peterborough on 60 Cromwell Road

Hussaini Islamic Centre on Burton Street Peterborough

The Heritage of the Community

Faizan-e-Madinah Mosque at Gladstone Street, Peterborough

New Ghousia Mosque at Gladstone Street Peterborough

The Heritage of the Community

UKIM Masjid Khadijah & Islamic Centre at Cromwell Road, Peterborough

Dar-as-Salaam Mosque on Alma Road Peterborough

The Heritage of the Community

Former Asian Cultural Centre Building on Lincoln Road, Peterborough

Gladstone Park Community Centre on Bourges Boulevard Peterborough
The Heritage of the Community

Nasar Ali, Ali Shauqat, Mohammed Riza and Muhammed Shazzad

The Heritage of the Community

Children in front garden in Cromwell Road in 1970,s

Gladstone Street opposite Link Road in 1970,

The Heritage of the Community

Cromwell Road in 1970,s

Taverners Road in 1980,s

The Heritage of the Community

Beeches Primary School in 1970's

Parents and Children Walking on Cromwell Road

The Heritage of the Community

Fish and Chips Shop on Corner of Gladstone and Hankey Street

Young children playing in front gardens

The Heritage of the Community

Children Crossing Road at Junction of Gladstone Street and Link Road

A young girl skipping in front garden

The Heritage of the Community

People in exodus from the old City of Mirpur

The Heritage of the Community

Minar-e-Pakistan in Lahore, built in commemoration of the Pakistan Resolution

Lahore Fort - UNESCO World Heritage Site

The Heritage of the Community

Faisal Mosque in Islamabad is named after the late King Faisal of Saudi Arabia

Shalamar Gardens in Lahore Constructed by Mughal Emperor Shah Jahan in
1642 - UNESCO World Heritage Site

The Heritage of the Community

The Badshahi Mosque in Lahore, commissioned by the Mughal
Emperor Aurangzeb in 1671 and completed in 1673

National Monument of Pakistan in Islamabad

The Heritage of the Community

Mirpur Cricket Ground

Regency Hotel in Mirpur

The Heritage of the Community

View of Mirpur City

View of Mangla Dam

The Heritage of the Community

View of Mangla Dam

View of Kotli

The Heritage of the Community

View of Kotli

View of Bhimber

The Heritage of the Community

Army training centre at Sarai Alamgir

Gujar Khan

The Heritage of the Community

Peterborough Cathedral

Peterborough Town Hall, Bridge Street

The Heritage of the Community

The Guildhall in Cathedral Square

Buckingham Palace, the home of the British Royal family

The Heritage of the Community

Peterborough City Centre in 1900

Russell Street in 1910

The Heritage of the Community

Beeches Primary School in 1900

Cromwell Road in 1900

The Heritage of the Community

Bridge Street in 1913

Lincoln Road in 1909

The Heritage of the Community

Triangle in New England in 1914

St Pauls Road in 1914

The Heritage of the Community

Allan Road in 1914

Craig Street in 1914

The Heritage of the Community

Rock Road in 1915

Padholme Road in 1920s

The Heritage of the Community

THE FIRST COUPLE: Nawabzada and Begum Ra'ana Liaquat Ali Khan

The Heritage of the Community

FAMILY PORTRAIT: With sons, Ashraf (standing) and Akbar

From left: Fazlur Rehman, Ghulam Muhammad, Liaquat Ali Khan, Quaid-e-Azam Muhammad Ali Jinnah, Ibrahim Ismael Chundrigar, Abdul Rab Nishtar and Abdul Sattar Pirzada

Sardar Mohammed Ibrahim Khan the first President of Azad Jammu and Kashmir

Quaid-e-Azam (Great Leader) Muhammad Ali Jinnah founder of Pakistan
with his sister Fatima Jinnah

Zulfikar Ali Bhutto the former Prime Minister of Pakistan

Prime Minister Nawaz Shriff on a foreign visit

Prime Minister of Pakistan Nawaz Shariff

Chuadhary Ghulam Abbas founder of
Muslim Conference Party in Jammu and Kashmir

The Heritage of the Community

Benazir Bhutto the former Prime Minister of Pakistan

The Heritage of the Community

Kalsoom Malik

This profile is from Kalsoom and it is entirely in her own words.

I was born and raised in Peterborough and am privileged to have followed a British educational path, setting a standard for the many coming generations of female born Pakistanis.

I have lived by the philosophy that nobody can take away your learning and my parents have encouraged me and my brothers to seek further education.

My parents were second generation Pakistanis to arrive in the UK. My father was a huge inspiration; having come to the UK as a teenager, he had gained an education and become a successful professional, graduate and officer with the Local Authority. My mother was able to read the Qur'an, but had never had any formal education. She was a big advocate for my independence and having the same opportunities to achieve success as my brothers.

I attended Queen's Drive West Infant School, All Saints CE VA Junior School, Deacon's School, where I gained GCSEs and A Levels, and The University of Nottingham where I gained a degree in Nutrition (honors): Second Class: Division One (2:1).

Following successful completion of higher education, I became a positive role model, giving other parents' confidence in their own daughter's potential. The acceptability of a university education for girls in my community increased as a result of myself and others of my age, successfully achieving degrees. We had shaped freethinking identities without renouncing traditional cultural values and practices.

I have worked full-time since my studies and gained other qualifications in my professional career, including an NVQ Level 3 in Health and Social Care, a Diploma in Counselling a Diploma in Psychotherapy and the National Professional Qualification in Integrated Centre Leadership (NPQICL) to support my current role in the management of a Children's Centre.

My cultural and religious obligations, have not hindered my professional aspirations. My qualifications, dedication and inherent desire for personal success have provided a foundation on which my professional career has been built. I value education and how unlimited the prospects are for an educated female and for a positive role model for others in the community.

Miss Nargis Sabir

Nargis was born and raised in Peterborough. She attended her local Gladstone primary school, Bretton Woods secondary school and Jack Hunt for sixth form A levels.

Later she went to the University of Leicester, where she gained a 2.1 degree in Psychology in 2013. Nargis said after graduating, she felt a sense of accomplishment and made her parents proud.

She is now employed by the National Health Service (NHS) in Kings Lynn as an Assistant Psychologist, working with young children with learning disabilities. She enjoys her job as it gives her a great satisfaction. This is her first employment after leaving university.

She continues to reside with her parents in Peterborough and her father is a well-known personality and a community activist in the British-Pakistani community.

About the British education system, Nargis said she believes that the British education is the best, most importantly, it is free, (although she is aware universities have different arrangements) and it offers opportunities' to achieve successes in your lives. She said that the education system has a good variety of options including paths to university as well as vocational qualifications and apprenticeships.

When asked about university experience, she said it was very different from living at home, as it gave her experience of independent living in a new and different environment, enabled her to meet new circle of friends, gave her confidence and experience to deal with many of the life challenges.

On education, her message to the members of the community is that any form of education is an investment and it is a link to your prosperity in life and said, "Education is a gift, which cannot be taken away and it pays the best dividends in life".

On Peterborough, Nargis said she has a lot of affectation for her birth City and the only city where she has lived all her life. She feels it is a wonderful, welcoming and cosmopolitan City and she is proud of her City.

Miss Nargis Sabir from Potha Bainsi, Mirpur

Mrs Rubina Ishrat Hussain MBE

Mrs Hussain was born in the Pakistani City of Lahore and she is a university graduate. In 1967, she married the late Haji Karamat Hussain of Potha Bainsi in Mirpur Azad Kashmir, a prominent community activist. In the same year of her marriage, she joined her husband in Peterborough.

Mrs Hussain's family home in Peterborough was located opposite The Beeches primary school and after her arrival in Britain and thanks to her husband for his encouragement and support; she quickly became a volunteer at the school. She promoted the school, encouraged parents to attend parent's evenings and she even provided interpreting services. Soon after, she was employed by the National Health Service (NHS), covering District Hospital and Maternity Ward employed as a paid interpreter. She worked at Neighbourhood House with Preschool children for many years. Later she worked at Deacons and Ken Stimpson secondary schools as a Language Teacher and Welfare Officer for several years. Mrs Hussain told me that she established a social get-together group for young Pakistan girls and worked at the project as a youth worker (part time) for several years. She also served on four different school governing committees.

In 1984, Mrs Hussain was appointed Justice of Peace (JP) for the Peterborough Bench and she served as the Magistrate for over 25 years. During that period, she was responsible for dispensing justice, based on fairness and equality. She was the first Muslim woman in Peterborough employed in a paid job and she was first Muslim woman Magistrate.

Throughout her life, she continued her involvement in the community and after dedicating decades helping the community, in 2006; she was awarded Member of British Empire (MBE) and After receiving an MBE, Mrs Hussain said she felt proud, valued and honoured that her contributions had been recognised in the queen's honours list.

On education, she said that a good level of education is essential for everyone as without it no one goes far or progresses in employment, promotion and career development.

Mrs Hussain remembers well when she first arrived in Peterborough in 1967 Peterborough was a small City to someone coming from the Punjab City of Lahore, it felt like a large village to her, although in recent years, the City has seen big changes due to the arrival of new migrants from Eastern Europe.

Mrs Rubina Ishrat Hussain MBE with her late husband
Haji Karamat Hussain of Potha Bainsi, Mirpur

The Heritage of the Community

Dr Ruqqayah Zafar

Dr Ruqqayah Zafar was born and brought up in Peterborough and attended local state-run schools, before attending university in a nearby city.

She said she was lucky that for her, her parents were supportive and encouraging, making an effort to attend parents' evenings and making sure that if she faced any obstacles, they did what they could to help her. For example, when she was rejected for a place on the A level maths course despite having acquired the prerequisite GCSE grades, her father took this up with the school until they were forced to change their decision. After her A levels, she obtained a place at her preferred medical school and at university, she did not face any problems or barriers as a result of her race.

On education, Dr Ruqqayah has said that her experience of the local education system was largely positive and she did reasonably well.

However, children of British-Pakistani background did face some extra difficulties during their schooling, which indigenous pupils would not necessarily encounter. Firstly, she thinks this has to do with many British-Pakistani parents not being entirely familiar with the British education system and what is required of them in supporting their children's education this is partly due to a language barrier and partly to apparent lack of interest. Both of these barriers are of our (i.e the British-Pakistani community's) own doing and if we want to change things we will have to address both within the community. In addition, she thinks that on the schools partly they did not always understand the background culture of their British-Pakistani students and as a result found it more difficult to relate to them.

She comes from one of the most respected families in the Peterborough British-Pakistani community and her father is a prominent community activist.

She is now a General Practitioner (GP), living and working in the Peterborough area.

Dr Ruqqayah thinks that Peterborough is a great place to live for many reasons, but thinks that the Muslim community has yet to realise its full potential.

Shama Akhtar

Shama was born in Peterborough in a British-Pakistani family.

She attended her local Gladstone primary school and Bretton Woods secondary school. She later went to Homerton College in Cambridge, where she gained a 2.1 degree in Religious Education (RE).

After graduating and qualifying with a PGCE, she was employed by William de Yaxley junior school.

Shama has been married for four years to Saqib - continues to live and work in Peterborough.

She is presently employed by the Thorpe primary school as Pupil Premium Project Manager.

According to Shama, she always wanted to become a teacher, even from an early age and she is pleased that her wish has come true.

She comes from a well-established and respected family all her three siblings are also graduates employed in respectable positions, her father is a well-known personality and a former Mayor of Peterborough.

Shama's view on education is that a decent level of education is an essential for everyone as it opens a new door and she is a strong believer that "education brings prosperity in life".

She has been involved with charitable causes in throughout life, including spending six weeks, along with her brother, in 2004 undertaking voluntary work on behalf of a British charity "Kashmir International Relief" teaching in six rural schools, spending one week in each school in Azad Kashmir. She also raised a considerable amount of funds for the charity through sponsorship.

Samoa is a strong believer in Trade Unions principals and values; she is a member of the NASUWT, The Teachers Union and is actively involved. She is the current President of the local Peterborough branch.

Her views of Peterborough are that she is proud of her City and the opportunities it has offered her and her family. She hopes to continue to live and work in the City and inspire others to achieve success in their lives

Yasmeen Javaid

I recently met Yasmeen and quickly learnt that she started life with a big disadvantage after struggling in her secondary school, but despite her education difficulties, she continues to sustain a normal life. This is her story as she told me.

Yasmeen was born in Peterborough into a British-Pakistani family. She attended Gladstone primary school, but during her time there, she relocated along with her family to Pakistan on a long stay. On her return to Peterborough, Yasmeen found secondary schooling difficult and constantly struggled; she ended up at the special school. According to Yasmeen she has made some further progress later on in her life

After leaving school, she held several factory jobs.

Just over four years ago, she married Iftikhar Ali; they now have a one-year-old daughter named Inayah Ali and the couple continue to reside in Peterborough.

On education, Yasmeen said, "education is essential to be able to live and survive in this day and age". On Peterborough, she said she is very proud of her City, as it is one of the most inspiring places to live a truly multicultural and peaceful city.

Yasmeen Javaid formally of Neeli, Mirpur carried by her mother
Khalida Bibi and standing with them is her older sister Rukhsana Kamar

References

The following sources were used in this book.

- Abdul Rahman: Early arrival experience
- British Broadcasting Corporation (BBC)
- CD Porsz - Pictures.
- Haji Mohammed Suleman: Early arrival experience
- Khalid Junvy: Chaudhry Fakeer Mohammed
- Internet Sites - Migration history, Reports on British-Pakistani Community
- Mohammed Nazir: Early arrival experience
- Muzaffar Hussain: Information on Masjid Khadijah & Islamic Centre
- Peterborough Images – Pictures
- Peterborough local History Society – Pictures
- Zahore Rahman: Information on Dar Assalaam

Remains of old Mirpur City under the waters of Mangla Dam

The Heritage of the Community

Raja Tahir Masood

Raja Tahir Masood was born in the small village of Morah Bari in the district of Mirpur in Azad Jammu and Kashmir, Pakistan.

He migrated to Britain at the age of 14 with his family and has ever since lived in Peterborough.

I have known Tahir for over 30 years. We first met when he was a sixteen-year-old voluntary youth worker at the Asian Youth Club. He was very passionate about his work and importance of the youth work. Even at that age, I could see in him the desire, enthusiasm and the commitment to work with young people and the community.

Later Tahir was employed by the Peterborough City Council as a community development officer working with the British-Pakistani community in Peterborough. He was based at the Gladstone Park Community Centre and we worked closely, initiating many new projects to meet the community needs.

Tahir went on to work for Peterborough City Council and Cross Keys Homes Housing Association in various officer positions for 20 years.

Tahir is friendly, considerate, hard working, likeable and determined man who is immensely proud of his Pakistani heritage - our community could do with more people like him.

Over the last few years, Tahir has undertaken some unique heritage work of great importance on the Peterborough British-Pakistani community, this pursuit is commendable and I am certain that his contribution are valued and appreciated by the Peterborough British-Pakistani community and his work will be recognised by future generations.

Nazim Khan MBE